Then, Suddenly—

Pitt Poetry Series

Ed Ochester, Editor

Lynn Emanuel

Then, Suddenly—

POEMS

University of Pittsburgh Press

Published by the University of Pittsburgh Press, Pittsburgh, Pa. 15261

Manufactured in the United States of America
Printed on acid–free paper
10 9 8 7 6 5 4 3 2 1

Library of Congress Cataloging–in–Publication Data and
acknowledgments are located at the end of this book.

A CIP catalog record for this book is available from the
British Library.

The publication of this book is supported
by a grant from the Eric Mathieu King Fund
of The Academy of American Poets.

In Memoriam

Akiba Emanuel

Camille Domangue

William Matthews

Contents

Then, Suddenly—

The book is the subject of the book.

—Edmond Jabès

Like God,

you hover above the page staring down
on a small town. Outside a window
some scenery loafs in a sleepy hammock
of pastoral prose and here is a mongrel
loping and here is a train approaching
the station in three long sentences and
here are the people in galoshes waiting.
But you know this story about the galoshes
is really About Your Life, so, like a diver
climbing over the side of a boat and down
into the ocean, you climb, sentence
by sentence, into this story on this page.

You have been expecting yourself
as a woman who purrs by in a dress
by Patou, and a porter manacled to
the luggage, and a man stalking across
the page like a black cloud in a bad mood.
These are your fellow travelers and
you are a face behind or inside these
faces, a heartbeat in the volley of these
heartbeats, as you choose, out of all
the journeys, the journey of a man
with a mustache scented faintly with
Prince Albert. "He must be a secret
sensualist," you think and your awareness
drifts to his trench coat, worn, softened,
and flabby, a coat with a lobotomy, just
as the train pulls into the station.

No, you would prefer another stop
in a later chapter where the climate is
affable and sleek. But the passengers
are disembarking, and you did not
choose to be in the story of the woman
in the white dress which is as cool and
evil as a glass of radioactive milk. You
did not choose to be in the story of the
matron whose bosom is like the prow
of a ship and who is launched toward
lunch at the Hotel Pierre, or even the
story of the dog-on-a-leash, even though
this is now your story: the story of the
person-who-had-to-take-the-train-and-walk-
the-dark-road described hurriedly by
someone sitting at the tavern so you could
discover it, although you knew all along
the road would be there, you, who have
been hovering above this page, holding
the book in your hands, like God, reading.

I am not at all the sort of person who attracts attention, I am an anonymous presence against an even more anonymous background. If you, reader, couldn't help picking me out among the people getting off the train and continued following me in my to-and-fro-ing between bar and telephone, this is simply because I am called "I" and this is the only thing you know about me, but this alone is reason enough for you to invest a part of yourself in the stranger "I."

—Italo Calvino

Out of Metropolis

We're headed for empty-headedness,
the featureless amnesias of Idaho, Nebraska, Nevada,
states rich only in vowel sounds and alliteration.
We're taking the train so we can see into the heart
of the heart of America framed in the windows' cool
oblongs of light. We want cottages, farmhouses
with peaked roofs leashed by wood smoke to the clouds;
we want the golden broth of sunlight ladled over
ponds and meadows. We've never seen a meadow.
Now, we want to wade into one—up to our chins in the grassy
welter—the long reach of our vision grabbing up great
handfuls and armloads of scenery at the clouds'
white sale, at the bargain basement giveaway
of clods and scat and cow pies. We want to feel half
of America to the left of us and half to the right, ourselves
like a spine dividing the book in two, ourselves holding
the whole great story together.

Then, suddenly, the train pulls into the station,
and the scenery begins to creep forward—the ramshackle shapes
of Main Street, a Chevy dozing at a ribbon of curb, and here is a hound
and a trolley, the street lights on their long stems, here is the little park
and the park stuff: bum on a bench, deciduous trees, a woman upholstered
in a red dress, the bus out of town sunk to its chromium bumper in shadows.
The noise of a train gathers momentum and disappears into the distance,
and there is a name strolling across the landscape in the crisply voluminous
script of the title page, as though it were a signature on the contract, as though
it were the author of this story.

The Book's Speech

As you are reading, you become the hard,
dark bulk looming at the end of a sentence,
you become the broken branch of lightning
falling and the groan of thunder, like an oncoming
migraine, and the flesh of your body pulls itself
closer, and behind you gathers a pressure of coats
and hats; you are now inside the crowd like an ache
in a tooth, that's you, muffled and woolly,
until a door opens to the tavern in the station.

You become a waitress. What does a waitress feel like?
What does it feel like to have a head like an airport fogged
in by a stout cloud of blond hair? You are picking up the
steins and saucers and there, amid the tinselly litter of the tavern,
is a dress like a plate licked clean. This clean wick, slick with beading,

is not a dress really, it is heartache-waiting-to-happen in
the train station of the small town where the rainy evening
is a window, black and shiny, where the passengers are
planted like flowers in the rubber pots of their galoshes.
And the train is coming, the train is surrendering under
a white flag of smoky hoots; the train is looking through
the dark with the big round lamps of your eyes, and above
you the moon looks like someone set her warm elbow
on a block of ice and left a cleft for your tongue to fall into.

The White Dress

What does it feel like to be this shroud
on a hanger, this storm cloud hanging
in the closet? We itch to feel it, it itches
to be felt, it feels like an itch—

encrusted with beading, it's an eczema
of sequins, rough, gullied, riven,
puckered with stitchery, a frosted window
against which we long to put our tongues,

a vase for holding the long-stemmed
bouquet of a woman's body.
Or it's armor and it fits like a glove.
The buttons run like rivets down the front.

When we're in it we're machinery,
a cutter nosing the ocean of a town.
Right now it's lonely locked up
in the closet; while we're busy

fussing at our vanity, it hangs there
in the drooping waterfall of itself,
a road with no one on it, bathed
in moonlight, rehearsing its lines.

Dressing the Parts

Here I comes.
—Anne Lauterbach

So, here we are,
I am a kind of diction

I can walk around in
clothed in the six–inch heels

of *arrogation* and *scurrility.*
And what are you

wearing? Is it those boxer
things again? I hope it is

those boxer things
and nothing else

except your eyes;
I like your eyes; do you

like the way my feet
are long, narrow,

with toenails like tiny television screens?
And hair is important.

A fog of hair floating
above the fields of the body.

Or the body as bald
as a truffle,

very French—
swine on leashes.

Like you, my pig,
I'm your truffle and

for you
reading is eating.

Is too.

When you were at the Brasserie
eating—

crêpes fourées, and,
légumes à la Grecque, and,

and, and—
you felt like you had read all of

Leaves of Grass at one sitting.
Wait, I see something

between your teeth:
it is a kiss as wet

and mobile as a gourami
in an aquarium.

Oh. God. Yes.
Describe the lips.

Describe what
the lips are wearing.

Is it that color called
Red-as-the-roofs-of-Brest?

That color that the lips
of the you are wearing?

That *you,* reader,
that you are wearing.

inside gertrude stein

Right now as I am talking to you and as you are being talked to, without letup, it is becoming clear that gertrude stein has hijacked me and that this feeling that you are having now as you read this, that this is what it feels like to be inside gertrude stein. This is what it feels like to be a huge typewriter in a dress. Yes, I feel we have gotten inside gertrude stein, and of course it is dark inside the enormous gertrude, it is like being locked up in a refrigerator lit only by a smiling rind of cheese. Being inside gertrude is like being inside a monument made of a cloud which is always moving across the sky which is also always moving. Gertrude is a huge galleon of cloud anchored to the ground by one small tether, yes, I see it down there, do you see that tiny snail glued to the tackboard of the landscape? That is alice. So, I am inside gertrude; we belong to each other, she and I, and it is so wonderful because I have always been a thin woman inside of whom a big woman is screaming to get out, and she's out now and if a river could type this is how it would sound, pure and complicated and enormous. Now we are lilting across the countryside, and we are talking, and if the wind could type it would sound like this, ongoing and repetitious, abstracting and stylizing everything, like our famous haircut painted by Picasso. Because when you are inside our haircut you understand that all the flotsam and jetsam of hairdo have been cleared away (like the forests from the New World) so that the skull can show through grinning and feasting on the alarm it has created. I am now, alarmingly, inside gertrude's head and I am thinking that I may only be a thought she has had when she imagined that she and alice were dead and gone and someone had to carry on the work of being gertrude stein, and so I am receiving, from beyond the grave, radioactive isotopes of her genius saying, take up my work, become gertrude stein.

Because someone must be gertrude stein, someone must save us from the literalists and realists, and narratives of the beginning and end, someone must be a river that can type. And why not I? Gertrude is insisting on the fact that while I am a subgenius, weighing one hundred five pounds, and living in a small town with an enormous furry male husband who is always in his Cadillac Eldorado driving off to sell something to people who do not deserve the bad luck of this merchandise in their lives—that these facts would not be a problem for gertrude stein. Gertrude and I feel that, for instance, in *Patriarchal Poetry* when (like an avalanche that can type) she is burying the patriarchy, still there persists a sense of condescending affection. So, while I'm a thin, heterosexual subgenius, nevertheless gertrude has chosen me as her tool, just as she chose the patriarchy as a tool for ending the patriarchy. And because I have become her tool, now, in a sense, gertrude is inside me. It's tough. Having gertrude inside me is like having swallowed an ocean liner that can type, and, while I feel like a very small coat closet with a bear in it, gertrude and I feel that I must tell you that gertrude does not care. She is using me to get her message across, to say, I am lost, I am beset by literalists and narratives of the beginning and middle and end, help me. And so, yes, I say, yes, I am here, gertrude, because we feel, gertrude and I, that there is real urgency in our voice (like a sob that can type) and that things are very bad for her because she is lost, beset by the literalists and realists, her own enormousness crushing her, and we must find her and take her into ourselves, even though I am the least likely of saviors and have been chosen perhaps as a last resort, yes, definitely, gertrude is saying to me, you are the least likely of saviors, you are my last choice and my last resort.

The Politics of Narrative: Why I Am A Poet

Jill's a good kid who's had some tough luck. But that's another story. It's a day when the smell of fish from Tib's hash house is so strong you could build a garage on it. We are sitting in Izzy's where Carl has just built us a couple of solid highballs. He's okay, Carl is, if you don't count his Roamin' Hands and Rushin' Fingers. Then again, that should be the only trouble we have in this life. Anyway, Jill says, "Why don't you tell about it? Nobody ever gets the poet's point of view." I don't know, maybe she's right. Jill's just a kid, but she's been around; she knows what's what.

So, I tell Jill, we are at Izzy's just like now when he comes in. And the first thing I notice is his hair, which has been Vitalis-ed into submission. But, honey, it won't work, and it gives him a kind of rumpled your-boudoir-or-mine look. I don't know why I noticed that before I noticed his face. Maybe it was just the highballs doing the looking. Anyway, then I see his face, and I'm telling you—I'm telling Jill—this is a masterpiece of a face.

But—and this is the god's own truth—I'm tired of beauty. Really. I know, given all that happened, this must sound kind of funny, but it made me tired just to look at him. That's how beautiful he was, and how much he spelled T-R-O-U-B-L-E. So I threw him back. I mean, I didn't say it, I say to Jill, with my mouth. But I said it with my eyes and my shoulders. I said it with my heart. I said, Honey, I'm throwing you back. And looking back, that was the worst, I mean, the worst thing—bar none—that I could have done, because it drew him like horseshit draws flies. I mean, he didn't walk over and say, "Hello, girls; hey, you with the dark hair, your indifference draws me like horseshit draws flies."

But he said it with his eyes. And then he smiled. And that smile was a gas station on a dark night. And as wearying as all the rest of it. I am many things, but dumb isn't one of them. And here is where I say to Jill, "I just can't go on." I mean, how we get from the smile into the bedroom, how it all happens, and what all happens, just bores me. I am a conceptual storyteller. In fact, I'm a conceptual liver. I prefer the cookbook to the actual meal. Feeling bores me. That's why I write poetry. In poetry you just give the instructions to the reader and say, "Reader, you go on from here." And what I like about poetry is its readers, because those are giving people. I mean, those are people you can trust to get the job done. They pull their own weight. If I had to have someone at my back in a dark alley, I'd want it to be a poetry reader. They're not like some people, who maybe do it right if you tell them, "Put this foot down, and now put that one in front of the other, button your coat, wipe your nose."

So, really, I do it for the readers who work hard and, I feel, deserve something better than they're used to getting. I do it for the working stiff. And I write for people, like myself, who are just tired of the trickle-down theory where somebody spends pages and pages on some fat book where everything including the draperies, which happen to be *burnt orange*, are described, and, further, are some *metaphor* for something.

And this whole boggy waste trickles down to the reader in the form of a little burp of feeling. God, I hate prose. I think the average reader likes ideas.

"A sentence, unlike a line, is not a station of the cross." I said this to the poet Mark Strand. I said, "I could not stand to write prose; I could not stand to have to write things like 'the draperies were burnt orange and the carpet was brown.'" And he said, "You could do it if that's all you did, if that was the beginning and the end of your novel." So please, don't ask me for a little trail of bread crumbs to get from the smile to the bedroom, and from the bedroom to the death at the end, although you can ask me a lot about death. That's all I like, the very beginning and the very end. I haven't got the stomach for the rest of it.

I don't think many people do. But, like me, they're either too afraid or too polite to say so. That's why the movies are such a disaster. Now *there's* a form of popular culture that doesn't have a clue. Movies should be five minutes long. You should go in, see a couple of shots, maybe a room with orange draperies and a rug. A voice-over would say, "I'm having a hard time getting Raoul from the hotel room into the elevator." And, bang, that's the end. The lights come on, everybody walks out full of sympathy because this is a shared experience. Everybody in that theater knows how hard it is to get Raoul from the hotel room into the elevator. Everyone has had to do boring, dogged work. Everyone has lived a life that seems to inflict upon every vivid moment the smears, fingerings, and pawings of plot and feeling. Everyone has lived under this oppression. In other words, everyone has had to eat shit—day after day, the endless meals they didn't want, those dark, half-gelatinous lakes of gravy that lay on the plate like an ugly rug and that wrinkled clump of reddish-orange roast beef that looks like it was dropped onto your plate from a great height. God what a horror: getting Raoul into the elevator.

And that's why I write poetry. In poetry, you don't do that kind of work.

Walt, I Salute You!

From the Year Of Our Lord 19**,
from the Continent of the Amnesias,
from the back streets of Pittsburgh
from the little lit window in the attic
of my mind where I sit brooding and smoking
like a hot iron, Walt, I salute you!

Here we are. In Love! In a Poem!
Slouching toward rebirth in our hats and curls!
Walt, I'm just a woman, chaperoned, actual, vague, and hysterical.
Outwardly, my life is one of irreproachable tedium;
inside, like you, I am in my hydroelectric mode.
The infinite and abstract current of my description
launches itself at the weakling grass. Walt, everything I see I am!
Nothing is too small for my interest in it.
I am undone in the multiplication
of my perceptions. Mine is a life alive with the radioactivity
of its former lives.

I am in every dog and hairpin. They are me! I am you!
All is connected in the great seethe of seeing and being,
the great oceans and beaches of speeding and knowing.

I groan and surge, I long for hatches and engine sumps,
for sailors in undershirts. Walt! You have me by the throat!
Everywhere I turn you rise up insurmountable and near.

You have already been every Conestoga headed to California
that broke down in a cul-de-sac of cannibalism in the Rockies.
You have been every sprouting metropolis rerouted
through three generations of industrialists.
You, the sweat of their workers' brows! You, their hatred of poets!

You have been women! Women with white legs, women with black mustaches,
waitresses with their hands glued to their rags on the counter,
waitresses in Dacron who light up the room with their serious wattage.
Yes! You are magically filling up, like milk in a glass, the white
nylon uniform, the blocky shoes with their slab of rubber sole!
Your hair is a platinum helmet. At your breast, a bouquet of rayon violets.

And you have been places! You have been junkyards with their rusted Hoovers,
the pistils of wilted umbrellas.
And then, on the horizon (you have been the horizon!)
Walt, you are a whole small town erupting!
You are the drenched windows. The steaming gutters.
The streets black and slick as iron skillets.
The tawdry buildings. The rooms rented.
And now, in total hallucination and inhabitation, tired of being yourself—
Walt, the champ, the chump, the cheeky—you become me!
My every dark and slanderous thought. Walt, I salute you!
And therefore myself! In our enormous hats! In our huge mustaches!
We can't hide! We recognize ourselves!

At the Ritz

How and where they met is cause for speculation.
All up and down the avenue, blondes—lacquered
in intelligence, sarcasm, babeness, and money—
gossiped into the ears of investment bankers
so impeccably groomed you could see them
checking their Windsor knots in the chrome
toes of their wing tip shoes.

He was so handsome that when he walked in
the room just rearranged its axis from south
to north, the scene came to a halt and hovered
as though the weight of him had tilted the planet
and everything was beginning a slow slide off.
Martinis tremble in their fragile glasses.
Against her mink a gardenia erupts in a Vesuvius

of white. These two haven't met. Until they do,
her job will be to pout beside her wealthy father who,
weighted with an enormous white mustache
(what brilliance: in this scene, hair is money),
is lying in the sedate and lacquered gleam of the coffin.
Above his stern but kindly visage some pricey
lilies droop. He's dead; she sulks.

But this is all a long way off. Now we're
at the Ritz where, as we've seen, the joint's atremble,
the tablecloths on the table so white, so limp,

they look like they have fainted. When he walks in,
she says, there is no here here, let's go down the street
to Izzy's. The street's grown quiet. Not even the moon
can move. Its grainy bulk, stolid and sinister at once,

won't budge. Behind them—the pale, small stares of the hotel
lobby, a taxi hauls a smudge of exhaust into place,
and a town staggers to its feet as he follows her like a prisoner
into the sentence of the story.

Nothing happens until something moves.

—Albert Einstein

Halfway Through the Book I'm Writing

This is the wonderful thing about art,
it can bring back the dead . . .

My father dies and is buried in his Brooks Brothers suit.
But I can't seem to keep him underground.
Suddenly, I turn around and there he is just
as I'm getting a handle on the train-pulls-

into-the-station poem. "What gives?"
I ask him. "I'm alone and dead," he says,
and I say, "Father, there's nothing I can do about
all that. Get your mind off it. Help me with the poem

about the train." "I hate the poem about the train,"
he says. But since he's dead and I'm a patient woman
I turn back to the poem in which the crowds have gone home
and the janitor pushes the big mustache of his broom across the floor,
and I ask, "Dad, is that you in there?"

"No, it's not."

A black cloud in the shape of Magritte's bowler,
plump and sleek and stark, hanging over the train station, says,
"I want to go to a museum; put one in the poem beside the station."

where it's morning and the ticket window is selling
tickets to a man in a hat and an enormous
trench coat, wrinkled and jowly, a woman

in white looks as cool as a martini in a chrome
shaker, a woman in red seethes in a doorway,
eager to become one of Those Beginning the Journey
and from the horizon's molten light the trains crawl out.

"And when I get to the museum I want to see
Soutine, Miró, Picasso, or Dali, I want eyes in my armpits
and my fingers, eyes in the air, the trees, the dirt."

"Father," I say, "you already are an eye-in-the-dirt."

It's early morning. In the pine tree I hear the phoebe's stressed
squeak, *fee-bee, fee-bay,* like the creak of the old guard at the museum
snoozing in his rocker before Soutine's still life of the butchered cows.

"Father," I say, "do you see them?"
And the phoebe says, Yes-squeak-
yes-squeak-yes-squeak-yes-squeak.

The Burial

After I've goosed up the fire in the stove with *Starter Logg*
so that it burns like fire on amphetamines; after it's imprisoned,
screaming and thrashing, behind the stove door; after I've
listened to the dead composers and watched the brown-plus-gray
deer compose into Cubism the trees whose name I don't know
(pine, I think); after I've holed up in my loneliness staring
at the young buck whose two new antlers are like a snail's
stalked eyes and I've let this conceit lead me to the eyes-on-stems
of the faces of Picasso and from there to my dead father; after I've
chased the deer away (they were boring, streamlined machines
for tearing up green things, deer are the cows-of-the-forest);
then I bend down over the sea of keys to write this poem
about my father in his grave.

It isn't easy. It's dark in my room, the door is closed,
all around is creaking and sighing, as though I were in the hold
of a big ship, as though I were in the dark sleep
of a huge freighter toiling across the landscape of the waves
taking me to my father with whom I have struggled
like Jacob with the angel and who heaves off, one final time,
the muddy counterpane of the earth and lies panting
beside his grave like a large dog who has run a long way.

This is as far as he goes. I stand at the very end
of myself holding a shovel. The blade is long and cool;
it is an instrument for organizing the world; the blade is
drenched in shine, the air is alive along it, as air is alive
on the windshield of a car. Beside me my father droops

as though he were under anesthesia. He is so thin,
and he doesn't have a coat. My left hand grows
cool and sedate under the influence of his flesh.
It hesitates and then . . .

My father drops in like baggage into a hold.
In his hands, written on my stationery, a note
I thought of xeroxing: *Dad, I will be with you,*
through the cold, dark, closed places you hated.
I close the hinged lid, and above him I heap a
firmament of dirt. The body alone, in the dark,
in the cold, without a coat. I would not wish that on my
greatest enemy. Which, in a sense, my father was.

The Instruction Manual

How-to on how to read this? Listen.
For one thing, there is no you.
She owns you: you're the dog;
she's the leash you follow

through the plot opening into the dark city.
The pace is frisky. To your left—door, door,
window, woman in red dress. You want,
in your doggy way, to back up to that hydrant

for a sniff. And to your right the throb of traffic.
You like her, but she likes Chevys
with glass-pack mufflers, the rickety staccato
of spiked heels nailing down the sidewalk.

Who is it? Wouldn't you like to know.
Plot doesn't tell,
that's what description is for.
It's clothing and it's revealing.
Listen to this: "the lissome friction
of the red silk dress is like a sea; you can hear it glisten."

Etcetera. You see with your ears, but
you aren't listening. You're a dog.
And you're lost. Where is my street, you wonder. Gone.
And so are you, you restless-longing-for-more.
Aren't you sorry. There is no more. No place.
Just blank page, white space, void with a splash of voice.

The Corpses,

hunched like poker players at my kitchen table,
under a seething stratum of cigarette smoke,
are unhappy

with the rewrites of the afterlife.
At their backs,
even the wallpaper

has a story to tell
about a few stout houses
in a bower.

Is bad taste catching? They want to know,
What's happening in this story?
Is the sea kissing up
to the shore? Are the whipped
egg whites of the clouds packed in the sky's refrigerator?

They are tired of being on artificial art support;
the corpses are tired of being used to prop open the plot.

A searchlight opens a sky.
This is the police,
bellow the police,
and the corpses stumble forward into a

dowsing of bullets.
They cannot escape me.
Even in death they have a faintly greasy,
slippery look. And even a corpse can be a disguise.

Persona

When the reader's radar tracked me down,
I had given up and become the dead man.
I throbbed in the big fog of his white shirt.
I called down the long tunnel of his throat
Oh dead man, where are we going? He called back—
Everybody is a door: Open: Enter: Become:

Then a door opened in the voluminous museum:
there he was standing in the hallway of his coat,
under a fedora so big and shadowy, so riven
with creases and valleys it looked like he was wearing
Mount Monadnock on his head. I shoved my head

into the mouth of his tragic hat, I donned
the trench coat with the lobotomy, and, just like
that, I was a man. On my finger I bore the tourniquet
of his ring, and I was happy inside my lonely
rayon blazer when a voice said suddenly—

LYNN EMANUEL, IS THAT YOU IN THERE?

No, I said, standing there clothed in the raiment
of a dead man. *No,* said the voice of the dead
man limping up and down the stairs of my voice.
No, No, No, said the voice of the dead man limping
down the long dark corridor of my throat.

In Purgatory

This is my usual room.
Beyond the window,
a lava flow of hot light,

Where is everyone, I wonder,
where, in particular, is my dead father
who should have been here

by now?
I'm watching the sunset climb,
rung by little rung,

the venetian blinds,
when a silky tickle
of road asks me—

Hey cutie, want to go
to the Big City?
No thanks!

reply the ladder backs
on the back stoop
with my grandpa's

thoughtful grumpiness.
Let's sit for a spell.
And so we do.

We sit and sit.
It's pretty spooky to see
my feet missing from the gas pedals

of the dark sedan parked before the boarding house.
Even my longing to be gone from here
is gone from here.

Painting the Town

I dip my brush into black.
Over a lip I build a black

mustache, a small dense
thundercloud, scented

with rum, sleek with waxes:
Husbands! And now,

awash in pale tresses,
holding their Pomeranians

on jeweled leashes: Wives!
Under the noses of presbyters

I compose grim gossiping.

Out of the eyelids of their daughters
grow awnings of lashes; the spikes

of their heels are driven like golf tees
into their lawns.

I open a vial of gunfire.

Out of the townspeople run
lush grottos of blood

into which my brush wanders
and reappears with a woman

in a red dress standing all alone
under the shaggy aster of a street lamp.

A Landscape in the Country

This thrust of eloquence is not
a Douglas fir, that nondeciduous blue-green talon.
It is an obituary, but mute.

Death. Woe. The nouns
stomp around the countryside in their burly boots.
The tree doesn't care

that its crumpled black, its suggestive cleft of shadow, the shape itself—all inlet—
is a harbor of green chop,
and a stand-in for Death.

The cows are another matter.
In their suffocating upholstery of black and white,
the cows are divans

with hoofs
perambulating around the meadow
to remind us of the fuggy parlors

of childhood
in Bolivar, Kansas.
So, of course, they stagger

under the weight of being the furniture
of desolate remembrance.
Never mind the cows;

against the bottom of the page,
that blank horizon, that palmy nothingness,
they are merely

the lowest stair in the stairway of Being
that we go down and down and down.

Soliloquy of the Depressed Book

Since I have come to hate Nature & its Poetry,
I hate every landscape pinned down by Scenery—
The Mountain Package, The Garden, The Vista
always flapping in my face;
I can't pour my broken heart into those rented rooms
with their tired aquatinted distances.
Don't be viewy, I think,
& soap shut the blue window of the sky.
I want machinery
to grind the mountains down to Mountain,
to drive the trees, like stakes, through the heart of The Glade.
I want images to inherit the earth
like kudzu spreading its ooze,
its mean replications, its malignant increase
over the landscape,
erasing the boundaries between itself & us,
between show & tell, master & slave,
until The World vanishes,
& we are left with an Image of The World.
Now every pane of glass in every window
is stenciled with images, even the doorknob,
like a tiny goldfish bowl,
is aswarm with them.
Every avenue of escape is closed.
Stop, say the red stop signs
that once were cardinals.
The wet & bloody pulp that once was Sunset seethes.
Night drags its glassy, abstract fingers

over the glassy abstract harp of Wind.
The World & I vanish into a dark
Image of The World-in-Darkness
which I remember was once merely
a mote in my own eye, a distant lark,
night on the dull horizon—
coming to serve me.

These Days,

in the teary windows, the woodlands heave
and twitch, and my neighbor, in her dark parka,
looks like a nail hammered into the fat upholstery
of the drifts. The silence clinks and clanks,
and my father's here as the endless task
that trickles down from the muses' mills
and shops. I have been bad. *Get back*
in the grave, for god's sake, Father! I tell him.
And he tells me, *I hate this poem about the fire.*

I never write from experience,
but halfway through the poem the fire bit me.
Just as I was feeding it the log that looks
like an autopsy performed on a telephone
pole, the fire turned on me like a sick dog.
Bitch. Bastard. What's fire's gender?
Bachelard says fire is the daughter of two
logs. Okay, so, I am writing a poem in
which I am peering down the long dark
road of a sentence and I hear my father saying
I knew a woman whose mind was like a
white veranda across which her thoughts
could glide in brilliant congress with one
another. Who are you dating?

The log I've named Gretel wells up dully,
her hair is a yellow fire struggling.
When it comes to Gretel, I am God.

I love the lush brocade of gray and black
the fire makes upon the logs. I am in favor
of the well-dressed. My dad looked great
buried in his tweeds from the Denver Junior
League. The snow, in drifts and bulging
hunks, reminds me of the casket's satin lining.
They snowplowed the dirt down on him.
I heard the roar of earth falling on the coffin.
I am pushing my luck with the stove. I just fed it a log
big enough to choke a horse. Even fire needs
a challenge. These days, what interests me most,
I can see, is the disappearance of matter.

3

Think of narrative from this thing, a narrative can give emotion because an emotion is dependent upon a succession upon a thing having a beginning and a middle and an ending.

—Gertrude Stein

She

The body has its own story   she said   Oh, yes?   I said.
The body   she insisted   doesn't care that it doesn't fit your theories   no I said   I suppose not
flesh, too, has a voice   and is quite articulate   it says—
yes I say   I know what it says   it says the end is the end   no matter how you slice it
precisely   she said   she was herself quite eloquent   we were sitting in the cafe   the street
disappearing behind the rainy plate-glass window   behind us hovered the waiter and the good smell
of coffee   she was beautiful   bookish   I loved her serious glasses   she was
trying to explain about the flesh   and I did not want to hear it   but   she persisted   your
stories   Yes?   utilize the latest methods   they disrupt everything!
strike out in new directions!   nothing is certain   death to tradition!   why thank you I said
at her back the city wept with rain   and to the dominant paradigm I said
death to the dominant paradigm   of the beginning the middle   all that sad etcetera
of course   she continued severely   the body is   I looked at her   her hair was long and as dark
as the earth and I said   of course   the body is   a thing having a beginning and a middle and an end
and is what my text struggles against   and so the body and I are like two people in a cafe   arguing about
the way the story would go   I argue my position vis-à-vis   the end and beginning   and the body argues
hers   yes   she said   but let's face it   no matter what you say   the body wins.

Elsewhere

This isn't Italy where even
the dust is sexual, and I am not
eighteen clothed in elaborate
nonchalance. C. T. Onions' *Etymologies*
says memory is related to mourning.
I'm always remembering myself
out of some plain place in the middle West,
some every-small-town-I-have-ever-hated-
and-grieved-my-way-out-of-in-poetry, chipping
the distance open with a train, awling
open with the train's hooting

a silence which is stolidly American, sturdy, woodsy.
Well, no, perhaps these woods are Dante's;
it's dark in here. I'm nearly fifty,
rummaging through the ruined beauty
of a girl at twenty who couldn't interrogate
her heart for more than five minutes.

—Just listen

even in Corsica where the repeated call of the
lighthouse throbbed like a piston, and the thin whine
of an engine garroted the quiet, and I stood good
as a flower in my pastel shirtwaist, poked and
nuzzled by my date, and listened to the mixing,
like a cocktail, of the water and earth, the cool
gargle, the slushy breathing of the surf, and
wished I were somewhere else

to her describing, even then, a longing
to escape. And, like me, she only does it on the page,
heaping up the elaborate scenery so
she can disappear into it.

On this flat EKG of horizon the silos are blips
repeating and repeating. There is a storm,
a thick, dark, hard knot of cloud, but it's stuck
in the chimney of my throat. Nearly fifty.

The fire is out, the cabin's dark,
and beyond, the woods are a platoon
of black trees. It's so quiet
I can hear my heart like the blows
of an ax, each blow blurred by an echo,

I can hear my heart inside my chest
trudging onward across the bleak tundra.
What was I thinking?

I look again at her poems flowing with
images, a restlessness, a terrible sense
of what's coming: She's writing me,
the woman she becomes, who could not
or would not save her.

In Search of a Title

I'm sitting on the porch, and the woods are still here.
Can't the trees do something besides vertical?
In *The Book Review* I read that nature is making
a comeback which is one more thing to make me feel
geeky and out-of–step. When's the literature
of boarded-up shore towns coming back? As usual,
I'm staring at the woods,

but the woods are a wall for turning sight away,
a blindfold across my mind. I stare at them as though
at the fire, or at the red coverlet across my closed eyes,
and disappear into the long hallway of myself where
Rachel Carson is saying, "If you understand nature,
you will never be afraid or alone." So, I've set myself
this small, unpleasant task: Describe the Tree as Though
You Like It. Today en route to the studio

a dogwood hovered above me, so thick and bright,
it was as though the woods had spun a ghost; its pale
and sloppily anthropomorphic form was more spacious
and more flexible than "Tree." Humble and penetrating.
Those are words that occur to me. Also, "dizzying
freshet," but I reject that in favor of something less
well-dressed. It's "spiffy" and "impudent." The tree
that is. That's why I like it. That white is a loose

shirttail. Does it seem like bragging to say it reminds
me of myself? I'd like to cast off Symbolisms—the need

to stuff Thought and Feeling into the strongbox of Nature.
What a giddy slosh of white ectoplasm the dogwood left
on that blue sky. I'd like just to proceed, strolling along,
side by side, as it were, immaculate, but unkempt. "White,"
occurs to me. And "Naked."

Homage to Sharon Stone

It's early morning. This is the "before,"
the world hanging around in its wrapper,
blowzy, frumpy, doing nothing: my
neighbors, hitching themselves to the roles
of the unhappily married, trundle their three
mastiffs down the street. I am writing this
book of poems. My name is Lynn Emanuel.
I am wearing a bathrobe and curlers; from
my lips, a Marlboro drips ash on the text.
It is the third of September nineteen**.
And as I am writing this in my trifocals
and slippers, across the street, Sharon Stone,
her head swollen with curlers, her mouth
red and narrow as a dancing slipper,
is rushed into a black limo. And because
these limos snake up and down my street,
this book will be full of sleek cars nosing
through the shadowy ocean of these words.
Every morning, Sharon Stone, her head
in a helmet of hairdo, wearing a visor
of sunglasses, is engulfed by a limo
the size of a Pullman, and whole fleets
of these wind their way up and down
the street, day after day, giving to the street
(Liberty Avenue in Pittsburgh, PA)
and the book I am writing, an aspect
that is both glamorous and funereal.
My name is Lynn Emanuel, and in this

book I play the part of someone writing
a book, and I take the role seriously,
just as Sharon Stone takes seriously
the role of the diva. I watch the dark
cars disappear her and in my poem
another Pontiac erupts like a big animal
at the cool trough of a shady curb. So,
when you see this black car, do not think
it is a Symbol For Something. It is just
Sharon Stone driving past the house
of Lynn Emanuel who is, at the time,
trying to write a book of poems.

Or you could think of the black car as
Lynn Emanuel, because, really, as an author,
I have always wanted to be a car, even
though most of the time I have to be
the "I," or the woman hanging wash;
I am a woman, one minute, then I am a man,
I am a carnival of Lynn Emanuels:
Lynn in the red dress; Lynn sulking
behind the big nose of my erection;
then I am the train pulling into the station
when what I would really love to be is
Gertrude Stein spying on Sharon Stone
at six in the morning. But enough about
that, back to the interior decorating:
On the page, the town looks bald

and dim so I turn up the amps on
the radioactive glances of bad boys.
In a kitchen, I stack pans sleek with
grease, and on a counter there is a roast
beef red as a face in a tantrum. Amid all
this bland strangeness is Sharon Stone,
who, like an engraved invitation, is asking
me, *Won't you, too, play a role?* I do not
choose the black limo rolling down the street
with the golden stare of my limo headlights
bringing with me the sun, the moon, and
Sharon Stone. It is nearly dawn; the sun
is a fox chewing her foot from the trap;
every bite is a wound and every wound
is a red window, a red door, a red road.
My name is Lynn Emanuel. I am the writer
trying to unwrite the world that is all around her.

Ode to Voice

How I love my eyes, dressed up
in the valences of their lashes,

staring out at the locust which
bats its flagelliform leaves at me.

Everywhere I look I see myself,
blunt and definite as this brick wall,

seething with repressed—
what?

Like me, the brick wall in its courses
wants to emulate the mobile,

the liquid loop of geese flung across
the sky, a sash undone from

the bulky kimono of the
firmament.

I love that firm word
for such a fuzzy and loose

experience as *sky*. But, anyway,
this narrow wall looking across

the narrow walk to my neighbor's house
is like the cover of a book. I'm the plot.

And I sit here staring out.
There is a locust tree and twenty chapters

in which
the locust, shaggy and flirtatious,

shuddering in the wind like a huge sea
anemone in the currents of the sea

stares back at me. Perhaps that's not
the whole story. Perhaps there is no story,

there's just a narrator, a voice perched,
like a finch on a leaf, between the end

and the beginning. I like that idea,
and, behind my eyes, so does my mind

which abhors it when
Things Happen

outside the glass-windowed
conservatory of the skull,

but loves the idea of a voice
like a leaf with a finch on it,

a voice like a sizzle
of something cooking

(we're cooking now, says
my mind thinking of bacon

in the silky black iron fry pan).
A voice is not a story but a way of

presiding over a story, if one
were to happen by.

It hangs in the closet
of the mind like a beautiful dress

waiting for a beautiful nakedness
to come along.

Portrait of the Author

Today I write about the house
of the body and about myself,

its shadowy proprietor,
coming and going.

Above the street, beside a fan
and a half-inch of bourbon

floating in a tumbler, someone's
white face pokes a hole

in a dark window. It's me,
in the body of a man named Raoul.

The rain stings the window
and the nothing beyond.

The rain throbs steadily
as the heart's dull return and lob.

Bending over the woman on the bed,
Raoul says, *Take off your dress.*

I'll take my dress off, the woman says.
And then the sibilant whisper

of a black silk frock.
(A what?)

Frock. On the floor.
Also hosiery. Also black.

Suddenly naked or wearing
only flawless technique

and the dark eyes of staring
breasts, the story ends

either (A)

Bending over her
beautiful and tragic face

against the pillows, Raoul says,
Oh Lynn, Lynn, you bring me to my knees.

or (B)

Gazing up into my own
beautiful and tragic face, I say,

Oh, Raoul, you bring me to my knees.

In English in a Poem

I am giving a lecture on poetry
to the painters who creak like saddles
in their black leather jackets; in the studio,
where a fire is burning like a painting of
a fire, I am explaining my current work
on the erotics of narrative. It is night.
Overhead the moon's naked heel dents
the sky, the crickets ignite themselves
into a snore, and the painters yawn
lavishly waiting for me to say Something
About Painting, the way your dog, when
you are talking, listens for the words Good Dog.

"Your indifference draws me like horses draw flies,"
I say while noticing in the window the peonies
throbbing with pulses, the cindery crows seething
over the lawn. "Nevertheless," I continue, "I call
your attention to the fact that, in this poem, what was
once just a pronoun is now a pronoun talking about
a peony while you sit in a room somewhere unmoved
by this. And that's okay. Gertrude Stein said America
was a *space filled with moving,* but I hate being moving.
If you want to *feel,* go to the movies, because poetry
has no intention of being moving; it is perhaps one
of the few things left in America that is not moving.

And yet, I am a fatalist when it comes to art
and orgasm in English, because in English
even a simile is a story and there is no trip
so predictable that some poem won't take it."
And just as I am finishing my lecture, here
is the snowy hem of the end of the page
and one of the painters says to me, "Actually,
I found that very moving. Get in the car.
I'll drive you home."

Then, Suddenly—

All bad poetry springs from genuine feeling.
—Oscar Wilde

Yes, in the distance there is a river, a bridge,
there is a sun smeared to a rosy blur, red as
a drop of blood on a slide. Under this sun,
droves of poetry readers saunter home
almost unaware that they are unemployed.
I'm tired of the dark forest of this book
and the little trail of bread crumbs I have
to leave so readers who say *garsh* a lot
can get the hang of it and follow along.
And so I begin to erase the forest and
the trees because trees depress me, even
the idea of a tree depresses me. I also
erase the white aster of a street lamp's
drooping face; I erase a dog named Arf;
I erase four cowboys in bolas and yet in
the diminishing bustle of these streets I
nevertheless keep meeting People-I-Know.
I erase them. Now I am surrounded by
the faces of strangers which I also erase
until there is only scenery. I hate scenery.
I wind rivers back on their spools, I unplug
the bee from the socket of the honeysuckle
and the four Black Angus that just walked in
like a string quartet. "Get a life," I tell them.

"Get a life in another world, because this is
a page as bare and smooth as a bowling alley,"
and, then, suddenly—renouncing all matter—
I am gone, and all that's left is a voice, soaring,
invisible, disembodied, gobbling up the landscape,
an airborne cloud of selfhood giving a poetry reading
in which, Reader, I have made our paths cross!

Acknowledgments

Versions of these poems, some with different titles, were published in the following journals: *The American Poetry Review* ("The Book's Speech," "The Burial," "The Corpses," "Dressing the Parts," "Elsewhere," "In English in a Poem," "Homage to Sharon Stone," "Ode to Voice," "Persona," "The Politics of Narrative," "She," "Then, Suddenly—," "These Days," "The White Dress"); *The Antioch Review* ("At the Ritz," "Out of Metropolis"); *The Boston Review* ("Like God," "Portrait of the Author"); *Boulevard* ("Walt, I Salute You!"); *Green Mountain Review* ("In Search of a Title," "Soliloquy of the Depressed Book"); *The Harvard Review* ("inside gertrude stein," "The Instruction Manual"); *Ploughshares* ("A Landscape in the Country," "Painting the Town"); *Parnassus* ("In Purgatory").

"Out of Metropolis" appeared in *The Best American Poetry 1994;* "Like God," appeared in *The Best American Poetry 1998* and in the 1998 *Pushcart Prize Anthology.*

"The Politics of Narrative" was published by the University of Illinois Press as part of a double volume which contained *The Dig* and *Hotel Fiesta.*

For their support, I would like to thank the Corporation of Yaddo and the MacDowell Colony, where many of these poems were written, and for their visions and revisions of this book, Maggie Anderson, Pat Dobler, Judith Vollmer, and Molly Peacock. And, for his support, I would like to thank Ed Ochester.

The paintings on the cover and the title page spread of this book are by the painter and sculptor Akiba Emanuel (1912–1993). The fourth of six children of Russian and Lithuanian immigrants, Emanuel was born in Scranton, Pennsylvania, and grew up in Toronto, Canada, and Rochester, New York. He left Rochester after graduating from high school and moved to New York City to become an actor with the legendary Yiddish Art Theater. In the years just before World War II, Emanuel traveled extensively in Spain, Italy, Vienna, Morocco, Egypt, Palestine, and France. In Nice, he met Matisse, for whom he modeled and with whom he studied during the fall of 1933. When he returned to the United States, he worked for the WPA and was part of the New York School of the 1940s and 1950s. His first one-man show, in February 1938, was in Marian Willard's East River Gallery, the precursor of the distinguished gallery that bore her name. With William DeKooning, Louise Nevelson, Joseph Albers, and Ad Reinhardt, he was a member of the group of painters which showed at the celebrated Artists' Gallery in Greenwich Village. The paintings in this book were part of a broad retrospective at the Alexander Gallery, New York, May 1994.

Library of Congress Cataloging-in-Publication Data

Emanuel, Lynn, 1949–
Then, suddenly— / Lynn Emanuel.
p. cm. — (Pitt poetry series)
ISBN 0-8229-4108-2 (cloth)
ISBN 0-8229-5709-4 (pbk.)
I. Title. II. Series.
PS3555.M34 T48 1999
811' .54—dc21 99-6655